To My Bearded Friend

"I could not endure a husband with a beard on his face . . ."

Beatrice, Governor of Messina's niece.
Much Ado About Nothing.

ISBN 0 9507277 0 9

Published by: Bolton Fine Arts
            (K. S. Tinning & Son Ltd.)
            2 The Crescent
            TAUNTON, Somerset. U.K.

Printed by: Barnicotts Ltd.,
             TAUNTON, Somerset.

To H, A and P.

Foreword

The idea of this publication came to me when, like millions of others, I decided to grow a beard. I was fed up with the daily shave, never quite managed to get the right results with electric razors and invariably nicked myself with conventional blades.

A well meaning friend tried to train me in the use of a cut-throat razor but the combination of my shaky hand and the vivid description of the weapon completely put me off.

Before launching my new growth, I thought it may be an idea to learn something about the subject and because my search for information was in vain, this small book was born.

Grateful thanks go to John Power for his splendid cartoons and for their help in typing and drawing I am indebted to Joan Farbus, Ann Gray and Julie Mitchell, none of whom are bearded.

Taunton   Keith Stewart

There was an Old Man with a beard,
Who said: 'It is just as I feared!
Two Owls and a Hen,
Four Larks and a Wren
Have all built their nest in my beard.

Limerick by and drawing after Edward Lear. From *A Book of Nonsense*, first
edition 1846

There was an Old Man in a tree,
Whose Whiskers were lovely to see;
But the Birds of the Air
Pluck'd them perfectly bare,
To make themselves nests in that tree.

Limerick and drawings by Edward Lear (1812–88)

Chapter 1

Beards – A Growing Fashion.

It is a fact that different subjects arouse passions in people, whether the subject be boats, flowers, cars, hats or toothpicks. Any subject can have its ardent enthusiasts–even beards–or especially beards.

It can be safely assumed that beards have as long a history as anything else made by man, so that the bearded can hardly be called a new cult. However, the rise and fall of the beard does not appear to get the recognition it deserves.

It has been estimated that there are some three million beard wearers in the U.K. alone. For these gallant individualists there has not, until now, existed a useful and economical source of reference, should they wish to learn the history, the purpose, the care and the treatment of the growth with which they have chosen to decorate themselves.

Perhaps decorate is not the correct word, since it depicts a certain femininity when applied to a person and a beard could hardly be considered feminine! However, it has been said that there is an element of art involved in the cultivation of a beard, with the result that a man may represent himself in many different ways, according to the shape, size and colour of his beard.

"... there is an element of art involved in the cultivation of a beard ... "

The splendid bushy white beard of Father Christmas conjures up the impression of kindness and generosity in anyone who may be similarly endowed. Contrast our friendly Father Christmas with the mysterious intrigue behind the short cropped "Goatee". Goatees are a special type of beard which resembles the tuft of hair growing from the chin of a goat. This style of beard has been popular in oriental countries and perhaps for this reason tends to be identified with mystery and intrigue.

"... a goatee resembles the tuft of hair growing from the chin of a goat ... "

There are numerous other images to be formed with the help of a beard and any aspiring don Juan need not be left out. If anyone should dare to criticise the practice of wearing beards, the most effective defence must surely be a rapid recitation of the most eminent human beings in almost every walk of life who were bearded. Shakespeare, Charles Dickens and H. G. Wells will suffice in literature. Bizet, Brahms and Tchaikovsky among many others in music. Numerous kings, nobles, presidents and sheiks plus historians, politicians, scientists and academics whose names would fill huge volumes.

The beard often serves as a form of trade mark and any advertising or marketing man worth his salt will know the benefits to be obtained from a distinctive logo. All major companies spend large sums inventing tortured initials or distorted emblems which look clever to them and which they think will make their company instantly recognised. Some examples of well known trade marks are shown here.

UBM LIMITED

CORRUGATED PRODUCTS LIMITED

STANDARD CHARTERED BANK GROUP

In this same way famous personalities can also employ their faces, suitably designed, to be unforgettable trade marks. We can cite Jimmy Hill, Clement Freud and the ubiquitous Rolf Harris as prime examples. In these cases the owner of the beard is instantly recognised. Similarly, beards tend to classify people. Everyone can recognise the "Stereotypes" shown here, appropriately adorned by a certain beard and hair-style.

Count Von Strangleheimer

Professor Bunsenbee

Johnny Dropout

Farmer Giles

In our time there is never a second thought given to the acceptability or otherwise of a beard, but it has not always been so easy, as we shall see. Over the centuries, bitter attacks on beard growers were regular features of life, sometimes launched by the Church and sometimes defended by the Church. At times they were the sign of the upper classes, especially when immaculately groomed, but the poor, no doubt, sported some pretty hefty and well populated specimens.

Perhaps we are at a time of least controversy over these facial accoutrements than at any time in history and this, together with the multifarious advantages detailed in the next chapter, will explain the present profusion of beards.

Chapter 2

Advantages and Disadvantages

Beard growers become pretty smug as they extol the virtues of their growths to anyone unwise enough to question them, but even so, it is doubtful that even the owners fully appreciate all the advantages.

The obvious one and the one most bragged about, especially in Winter, is the Time Saver. The importance of it is most appreciated in the morning when the poor long suffering beardless chap has to be up those five minutes earlier to shave. How we gloat over those valuable minutes as we snuggle in our beds!

". . . we gloat . . . as we snuggle in our beds . . ."

Another advantage, of course, is the Money Saver. The cost of razor blades, shaving soap and the wear and tear on the brush (and nerves if a cut throat razor is used) must all be counted, or for those who are mechanised, the cost of electricity and depreciation of the machine.

When the beard gets long enough, you may even risk going without a tie and eventually your beard may even double as a scarf. This advantage could be considered both time and money saving.

"... eventually your beard may double as a scarf ..."

Now imagine the biting northerly wind tearing at your face if it has no protection and a further advantage becomes obvious, especially for outdoor workers such as farmers and builders. Let us call this one the Face Saver. "Ah!"

defiantly shouts the smooth-faced doubter, "What about the heat of Summer?", but we have further benefits emanating from our cultivated growth even in the Summer months. Many people suffer from a virus which is activated by the sun's rays which often causes blisters on the lips and elsewhere on the face. A suitably grown beard can prevent such an occurence and it has, in fact, been so proven. As for the heat, can anyone think of a more efficient system of refrigeration than a cold water sponge attached to the face?!"

So, after the Blister Saver and the Sweat Saver, we come to the Scar Saver. Some people during the course of their lives have had the misfortune to suffer an injury to some part of their face which has left an unsightly scar. In some cases there may be a small birthmark. Although unimportant to others, the bearer may feel uneasy about it. For those unduly conscious of their blemishes, a beard is the perfect cover up.

Apart from the previous advantages, there is one which few beard owners would be sufficiently immodest to admit. I refer to the dignity and additional authority which a well kept beard attracts to its owner. It makes an ordinary face become distinguished and important and a casual glance through any history book will confirm this.

The disadvantages are fewer in number and of less importance but must be noted lest the reader should suspect the author of prejudice.

Some disadvantages may be interpreted by confirmed beard owners as advantages. For example, when eating a particularly succulent meal, one is apt to slurp a little gravy on the beard and if it is somewhat greasy it may be difficult to remove before your next hot shower. In this way the memory of a good meal can linger on.

". . . one is apt to slurp a little gravy . . ."

A similar experience may occur with frothy beer although a supple tongue can usually deal with this problem satisfactorily, even pleasurably.

". . . frothy beer can be dealt with satisfactorily, even pleasurably . . ."

Of course, a beard does require a certain basic maintenance. This is not a great disadvantage to the initiated, since it must be remembered that true beard owners become very attached to their growths indeed. Thus they tend them as a gardener might tend his favourite plants and the trimming becomes a moment of joy instead of a chore. Expert advice and assistance is at hand when you make your regular visit to the barber and his professional fees are most reasonable.

". . . beard owners become very attached to their growths . . ."

Chapter 3

Its Birth and Upbringing

The birth of a new beard is probably the most difficult time for the man who cares about his appearance. We all know how untidy an unshaven face can look after one or two days, before it is obvious that the growth is intentional and not the result of mere lethargy or poverty.

Many successful beards were conceived during a few days illness or during a holiday well away from one's usual acquaintances. If such an opportunity does not present itself and you are reticent to take the plunge, it may help to wait for a single bank holiday which falls on a Friday or Monday, thus giving three clear days start. If you make sure not to have any important appointments on the last working day before the holiday, you can get away without shaving for that day, thus providing four days of growth before facing the ordeal of introducing your new acquisition to your workmates and colleagues, so that, although it may be far from beautiful, at least it will be obvious by then that the

". . . As your beard grows, your resolve to keep it will also grow . . ."

"dirty smudge", as it will doubtless be called, is intentional.

As the beard grows, your resolve to keep it will also grow, but do not expect any praise or flattering comment before the third or fourth week. After one month the constant flow of insults will gradually subside. Then, as the number of comments of approbation increase, a large number coming from the fairer sex, you will notice an occasional defection of a clean shaven to your ranks.

It is important to advise you to suppress, as far as possible, the urge—the insatiable urge, to scratch during the first weeks. Not only will the clean shavens obtain a devious pleasure from your discomfiture, but the ladies may withhold their words of encouragement in the mistaken belief that some alien creatures have taken up residence in your beard.

". . . it is important to avoid the urge to scratch . . ."

Consideration will have to be given, in due course, to the type of growth to be cultivated. This depends entirely on the wishes and personality of the owner, but a few general rules may be in order here.

Contrary to expectations, a thin face is still recognized as such even when covered with hair and similarly a fat round face continues to have that appearance with or without a beard covering it.

However, a part beard can successfully alter the shape of the face but unfortunately will continue to require the attention of a razor. Some of the illustrations in this chapter will clearly demonstrate how a face can be altered. (I would not presume to say improved, as that depends on the opinion of the beholder.)

Whether or not the result is worth the loss of one of the main advantages, that is, those extra minutes in bed, is entirely up to the owner.

Some beards turn out to be multicoloured, perhaps brown, red and grey. Others may be totally black or almost all grey, much to the surprise of the owner who may not otherwise possess a grey hair in his head. Such surprises need not daunt you, but be turned to advantage either by the clever manipulation of trimming scissors so that the emphasis is placed where required or else some skilful dyeing as was common practice at one time.

Regular grooming is a necessity if you want to retain a respectable appearance. No effort is required to look like a tramp. Just let your hair grow everywhere, on your face, head, neck and down your noise, if it is so inclined. To avoid the appearance of a member of a lost tribe, basic maintenance and upkeep with comb and scissors is a minimum requirement. Whenever you comb your hair in the mirror, remember your beard too. How could you forget, you ask, if you are looking in a mirror? However, a well matched beard can blend so well that it can be overlooked, unless you get into the habit of quickly dragging your comb through it.

". . . no effort is required to look like a tramp . . ."

Trimming is very important. As a rough guide to the frequency with which a beard should be trimmed, I would advise that action be taken when you find yourself chewing strands of moustache with your food. Small scissors are recommended for this purpose as they are light and easy to manipulate and any errors are unlikely to be fatal. Practise may be needed with the left hand to trim both sides effectively but if this proves to be an insurmountable problem you may care to take a chance and ask for assistance from your wife or girlfriend. It may be wise to check over your insurance policies before they rush to your assistance. However, the soundest advice by far is to entrust your treasured possession only to an experienced barber.

". . . practice may be needed to trim both sides . . ."

For those who have become addicted to their beards and would like to experiment in some of the hallowed rituals of beard care practised in bygone years, we should include in this chapter some helpful hints and tips on the care, preservation and beautification of the beard which were used by some of our predecessors. Many centuries of experience have gone before us and left a legacy of shrewd practice to maximise man's bearded plumage such as would put a peacock in the shade. Although practically impossible to find today, one could once buy in the shops a small beard brush and comb and a perfumed wax as a necessary accompaniment. Beards were regularly dyed and the "does he or doesn't he?" game was mostly played by women.

In spite of the varied perfumes, dyes and waxes for the do-it-yourselfer, trimming was usually left to the professional barber and often the dyeing would also be carried out by him at considerable expense.

Other select beard treatment included splashing with rose water or lavender with sugar. The aromatic embellishments were limitless. Presumably, anyone particularly partial to the odour of any one thing from garden mint to aniseed could practise self indulgence by soaking the beard in the appropriate substance. This practise may well point to a relationship between the vast consumption of scotch whisky and the proliferation of beards in Scotland.

". . . aromatic embellishments were limitless . . ."

Bearded persons with a more artistic bent as opposed to the culinary types may appreciate the comments of a barber earlier in this century. He remembered "Glorious grizzled ornaments of lovely hues of red . . . The red beard never attained its beauty unless allowed to grow wild. The wild dense growth of a full beard gave colour and lent distinction to the owner."

Touching up the beard with nitrate of silver to darken it can be resorted to, giving it an irridescent rainbow effect when struck by the sun's rays. Chloride of gold was used to obtain a brownish colour but with the same result in sunlight as nitrate of silver. Modern dyes are doubtless easier and safer but far less exciting.

Chapter 4

The History of Beards

Since shaving cannot be considered a natural thing to do, it must be assumed that beards go back as far as man existed and, indeed, Adam is traditionally depicted with a beard. In searching for additional evidence of beard popularity, we can easily find plenty of kings, deity, nobles and famous men over many centuries who have refused to be parted from their facial hair. Royalty has always shown itself to be particularly partial to beards.

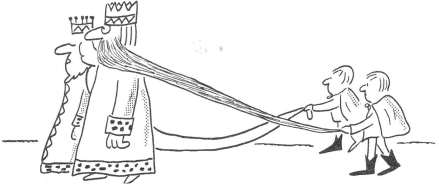

". . . Royalty has always shown itself to be particularly partial to beards . . ."

By historical standards we are now a very conservative breed of beard wearer. The ancient Egyptians used to have their beards frizzed, dyed and sometimes braided. A very emminent beard such as a royal one could be braided with gold thread. It may be said that the beards went to their heads, since they would wear a false metal beard or "postiche" as a sign of their status. Even the queens tried to be recognised in this way, tying a false beard to their chins with a head scarf or ribbon. It seems that "women's lib." arrived long ago.

Greeks tended to wear curly beards, while the tidy Romans would maintain theirs neatly trimmed.

Coloured people, as may be expected from the climatic regions to which they customarily belong, do not usually grow as much hair as whites.

The American Indians would pluck every hair from their face and body, but some African tribes treated a beard as a sign of manhood.

The religious significance of the beard over the centuries has been profound and contradictory.

Mohammed asked his followers to grow beards and both the Jewish rabbis and the Eastern Orthodox priests traditionally feature extravagant beards. According to the Orthodox view, the beard belongs to the "image of God" and shaving is thus viewed as a desecration of the image of God.

The very basis of Sikh tradition and doctrine involves unshorn hair, which presumably includes his beard, and any of the "Khalsa" who cuts off his hair is a renegade. However, Hindus are usually clean shaven as were the Christian clergy in this country except for a while in the 7th century when they were forbidden by law to shave.

If we go back in history as far as the Barbarians (500–1100) we learn that the British Catholic priests were squabbling with the Holy See in Rome over whether or not they should be shaved. The British priests were against shaving but the Pope considered it to be essential for salvation and finally ruled that the priests must not wear either beard or whiskers.

The numerous bans on beards indicate that they were never completely obeyed. In 1073, Pope Gregory issued an edict forbidding the clergy to wear beards. The Archbishop of Rouen proclaimed that anyone wearing long hair or a beard should be excluded from the church "both before and after death".

The importance of beards was not lost to Royalty, however, for a charter made at the time and still in existence was sealed with the addition of three hairs from the king's beard.

In the sixteenth century, there was a strong beard cult. This was doubtless due to the influence of at least two bearded monarchs. Stories of beards abound in European history books.

An 8ft 9in. beard on display in the Museum in Braunau, Austria, belonged to a local burgemeester who met his untimely death by tripping over his beard and falling down the stairs of the council chamber.

In France in 1535, was issued the very unjust edict of Beards, which forbade anyone from appearing in the Hall of Justice with a long beard. There are several instances on record of bearded persons being refused justice until they had removed their beards.

"... bearded persons were refused justice until they had removed their beards ..."

In the 19th century there was always considerable controversy about beards. The rather unwieldy title of one book was "Beard Shaving and the Common Use of the Razor; an Unnatural, Irrational, Unmanly, Ungodly and Fatal Fashion among Christians". This was followed within a few years by another entitled: "Shaving, a break of the Sabbath and a Hindrance to the Spread of the Gospel".

An article in the London Methodist Quarterly Review quoted an earlier Christian Father who claimed that Christ himself was never seen in a painting without a beard and that "to shave the beard is blasphemy against the face".

In the latter half of the 19th century and first half of the present one, various oddities appeared including the "mutton chops". In some instances, the mutton chops were allowed to almost meet at the chin, whilst in others, a clear expanse of chin would be kept clear of hair. In the latter case, perhaps we could hardly call the growth a beard.

During the two world wars of this century, beards suffered a great setback. Not unnaturally, beards were not permitted in most of the Armed Forces; the trench conditions perhaps being conducive to a rapid breeding of lice, although the additional protection from the cold would have been very welcome for some soldiers. Between wars, and since the last world war, we have seen a rapid return of a variety and profusion of hairy faces. This may be partly due to new shampoos and a general raising of standards of hygiene.

". . . a general raising of standards of hygiene . . ."

The beard, it seems, is currently very much in favour.

Chapter 5.

Types of Beards—
Past, Present and Future

1. Past.

Beards have such a long history that the sheer variety of shapes and sizes and, possibly, their weight is quite staggering.

We show here some of the styles which have been popular in the dim and distant past and one must be impressed with the time and care spent on them. Most probably, men's facial growths occupied as much time then as ladies' hair styles do now, if that is possible!

Evidently, no expense was spared for these creations. The decline in the use of gold thread may be excused at today's prices but like old buildings or fine old masterpieces, painstakingly made by master craftsmen, it would seem that we have seen the last of those magnificently sculptured beards.

Persian

Assyrian King

Greek

More recently but still very much in the past, beards became perhaps less exotic but possibly more meaningful and, at least, we are able to put descriptive names to a large number of styles.

Long Forked

Sugar Loaf Beard

Cathredral Beard

Swallow Tail

Stiletto

Mutton Chops

Saucer Beard

Miners Beard

2. Present.

Although today's beards do not have the decorative appearance or colourful names of days gone by, perhaps the sheer quantity compensates for this. We seem to meet beards everywhere we go and everywhere we look, whether it be on the television, cinema, behind shop counters, on building sites, in the stockbroker belt and on farms (apart from the goats!).

Generally speaking, they are a fairly conservative lot, some shorter, some bushier, but not a forked beard nor a swallow-tail beard to be seen anywhere.

Where are today's adventurers? Where are the innovators and extroverts of yesteryear? Today's beards appear to be limited to common bush beards, a few square cut beards, a few half moons and various hybrids.

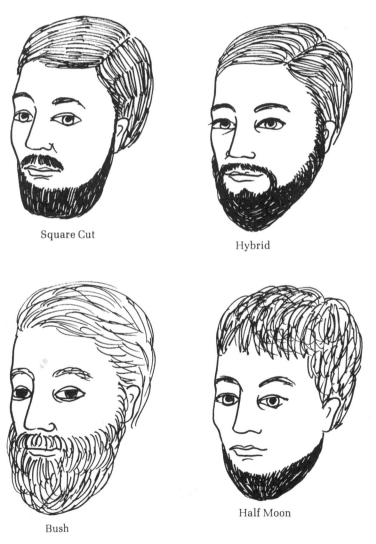

Square Cut

Hybrid

Bush

Half Moon

Let us hurry on to the future to see what may be in store.

3. Future.

With the advent of new technology, new words have had to be invented to enable us to describe the new inventions and never has the world known such rapid and far reaching changes in almost every walk of life.

Who can say that this growth in scientific knowledge will not be matched by growth in beard styles, appropriately named.

"...the advent of new technology has not been matched by new styles..."

The time for futuristic beards is upon us and I shall be pleased to lead the way with a few hoary suggestions for updating those hairy accompaniments.
Here are some ideas:

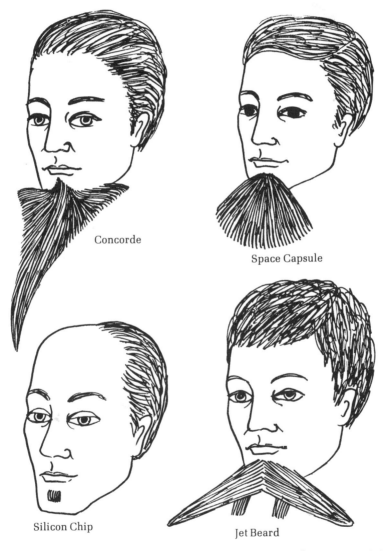

Concorde

Space Capsule

Silicon Chip

Jet Beard

It seems that a national or international competition should be organised to goad bearded men into inspired action with scissors, curlers, wax and combs. What an ideal television programme it would make and so perfectly suited to the small screen. "Bearded Mr. Universe" where are you?

Chapter 6

Other Excrutiatingly Interesting Facts about Beards

If you care to look up the word "barber" in the Concise Oxford Dictionary, you will see that he is described as "a person who shaves and trims beards and hair". The surprising thing about this description is that the beard is given prominence over the hair. This may be because "barber" comes from the latin "barba" meaning beard and the same word and meaning continues in Spanish to this day.

The Royal Navy has a great tradition of beards but it must be a "full set" and anything less, such as a moustache, is strictly forbidden. Our own Prince Charles could not resist the temptation to sport a "full set" when he completed his training as a captain and took command of a Royal Navy Minesweeper, but he risked being relegated to the ranks when he appeared for a day with only half of his creation having been demolished. Fortunately the remainder, his moustache, quickly disappeared and saved many embarrassed faces, bearded and otherwise

The Guinness Book of Records tells us that the longest preserved beard was 17 ft (5.2 metres) and is still on view at the Smithsonian Institution, Washington D.C. without its originator, who departed our world many years ago. Anyone trying to beat this record should heed a word of advice: Take care when zipping up your anorak.

The text in the showcase reads as follows:–

A man's beard—a secondary sex characteristic—potentially can grow as long as his head hair. Individual hairs of Caucasoids—in whom the growth potential is greatest—seldom exceed 12 inches.

Hans Langseth (1846–1927) of Barney, North Dakota, took 51 years to accumulate the record beard shown here. It was achieved by a process in which the hairs that had been shed became matted. (Root ends throughout the matted portion prove this.) Stretched out loosely, the beard measures 17 feet; it can be stretched to about 19 feet. His was a rare form of body decoration.

United States National Museum of Natural History, Smithsonian Institution, Washington D.C. 20560.

Beards have been known to be used for smuggling but it must be admitted that anything larger or heavier than a golf ball would not be easy to conceal beneath the average facial undergrowth. Nevertheless, diamonds, drugs, gems and even coded messages can all be carried unsuspectingly by an innocent looking beard, and customs officers have learned to cast a professional and, no doubt, critical eye at all suspicious looking beards.

"... customs officers cast a professional eye at suspicious looking beards ..."

The Blue Peter television programme showed a public spirited gent with only half a beard. This had been grown with the perfectly legal, even admirable, idea of raising money for a worthy charity. The resulting success proved that even half a beard can be better than none.

Through the ages, man has invented many useful and useless objects but my investigations failed to reveal any beard training or grooming devices worthy of merit.

An odd shaped cup invented in 1872 was intended to make eating and drinking easy without polluting the beard or moustache but such an object could be made superflous by any spoilsport merely by trimming any excess hair around the mouth.

A German gentleman invented a very uncomfortable looking moustache trainer but perhaps because he failed to fire the imagination of the masses with it, nobody has bothered to turn any creative genius towards the betterment of beards.

Beards are always good conversation pieces, especially or perhaps only, among bearded gentlemen and you should not feel inhibited in ringing the changes if you are so inclined, adding ammunition to the dining room chatter.

A change is as good as a rest and a change of style will inevitably bring a chorus of comment, not always flattering. A veteran beard owner will be hardened to any cutting commentary, if that is the correct adjective and is always receptive to praise.

I can recall a middle aged gent who grew his first beard in his late thirties and everyone constantly and unkindly reminded him of how it aged him by at least five years.

When he eventually succumbed to their barracking and removed the growth, his friends marvelled at how young he looked and estimates ranged from ten to fifteen years younger! Ever since, he has taken to growing a beard for six months every two years in order to knock at least five years off his age each time.

Superstition sometimes associates itself with a beard. The world champion tennis player Bjorn Borg never shaves during the Wimbledon fortnight and this simple strategy has won him the title a record five times. Some simple minded people think that he won because he is the best player but surely that must be coincidence.

It must be conceded, however, that these tactics are not appropriate for all sports. Mike Brearley captained the England Cricket XI to victory over Australia when he was clean shaven, but when he failed to wield his razor in the Test Match in Australia in 1979, allowing a substantial growth to commandeer his face, he also failed to wield the cricket bat satisfactorily and England was humiliated in a 3–0 result. Ian Botham the new Captain and several other test cricketers have refused to see anything ominous in Mr. Brearley's experience and are sporting their own fuzzy facial designs. Perhaps such beards could be turned to advantage on the cricket field, after all.

". . . beards may be turned to advantage . . ."

If the day arrives when you decide to banish the beard completely, remember to take a photograph of it for posterity and so that you can gaze at it with nostalgia in your old age.

May it never enter your head to wonder how you ever had the courage or conceit or feeble-mindedness to let yourself be seen in public with such an ugly, unruly appearance!

To Beard or Not to Beard

To beard, or not to beard: that is the question:
Whether 'tis nobler for the face to suffer
The stings and scars of bladed torture,
Or to stand firm against a sea of critics,
And by opposing end them? Awake, asleep,
No more to face the ragged razor's edge;
The unnatural tearing from the roots
Of living whiskers. Tis a consummation
Devoutly to be wished. A beard: ah, yes;
A beard, envy of all: ay, there's the rub:
For in that thought of it what dreams may come
Of looks and fortune, dignity and fame.
It gives us pause. There's the respect
That becomes humility from laughter;
For who would bear the grins and scorn of friends,
Their sarcastic wit, the proud man's contumely,
The pangs of dispriz'd love, the sore delay,
The insolence of office, and the spurns
That patient waiting for the growth takes
When one himself might his quietus make
With unsheathed blade? who would fardels bear,
To grunt and sweat under prickly stubble,
But for the hope of something before death,
That undiscover'd country from whose bourn
No traveller returns, perish the thought.
Rather face the world with hairless chin
Than weaken after sprouting begins.
Thus critics do make cowards of us all;
And thus the native hue of resolution
Is sicklied o'er with the pale cast of thought,
And thus enterprising beard growers do pause
And from hirsute pursuits turn away,
And lose the name of action.

J. Farbus

(With apologies to the Bearded Bard.)